Monet's Garden

Monet's Garden

by

Susan Skinner

HEADLAND

British Library Cataloguing in Publication Data

Monet's Garden: poems by Susan Skinner

ISBN 0 903074 63 X

First Published in 1991 by HEADLAND PUBLICATIONS

38 York Avenue
West Kirby,
Wirral
Merseyside L48 3JF

ACKNOWLEDGEMENTS

Acknowledgements are due to the editors of the following magazines in which some of these poems first appeared: Orbis, Outposts, Weyfarers, A Mirror to our Day, Owl, Nursery World, The New Writer, The Woman Journalist, Vision On.

Typeset in Great Britain by Microbiz, London. tel 071-739 1292
Printed in Great Britain by Piggott Printers Ltd, Cambridge. tel. 0223-350131

In Memory of My Father

Contents

(Cont.)

Contents (Cont.)

Light a Candle

Monet's Garden

Summer at Giverny, red fish swim
in a reflected garden, flower and fern
their speckled heaven; flick a downward path
through shades of green to dark hypnotic depths
that mingle earth and sky and may alert
the drowning upside down world of the heart.

Paintings draw us to those depths, return
us to this quiet room in the museum
where Monet puts his finger on the soul.
Winds scallop water, willows trail,
long shadows graze, a wild hedge
of colour overgrows the painter's bridge.

They say he was becoming blind: his sunlights
spray like surf on leaves, burnish the white
lilies in his pool. Impressions float
easily and yet his vision sets
a stillness on the rainbow sun and makes
a beauty of all things that flower and break.

Bonfire Night

Before the guy is burned when fireworks
make us sigh, they come, old men
with lurching wheelbarrows, to dump
their autumn debris on the downs.

Others at nightfall make the pile
grow, mushroom like - tradition has it -
near the '*No Rubbish*' sign. But who
should label these delapidated

secrets, rubbish? - all that's left
of lost and summer days - a chair
it's woven seat in rags, it's sitter
present and no longer there.

A melted photograph, a box
half sealed, a mattress stained with age.
One curled up walking boot, and where's
the bird who flew this rusty cage

and left his singing in the air?
Tonight winter begins. The frost
is clean and clear, the children crowd
with all the childhoods from the past

to watch the startling fireworks rise
and Guy Fawkes stuffed with newspapers
float into flame, while overhead
the universe burns up like stars.

The Astronomer

Telescoping light,
the pale astronomer
observes a sky in flight.

Universes stir,
flair and black and die
along the centimetre

of his lonely eye.
Space that never sleeps,
all the leaping sky,

draw him to the deeps,
the dark where time began.
He watches and he weeps

who contemplates that span,
who meets the eye of night,
the measurement of man.

Photographs from N.A.S.A.

The photographs from N.A.S.A
are not about space,
but Christmas trees.
The universal blackness
branches everywhere,
bearing little worlds
round, clear and shining
like Christmas tree baubles.
They glitter perfectly
with self-contained light,
bringing a strange message
of hope and celebration.
As if the blackness
they cannot illuminate
is lit up in some other way,
too awesome for light.

The Return

Orion stands, bold, triangular,
like an Egyptian figure,
three jewels in his belt.
Pleiades, the veiled women
whisper in their black court
as Halley's comet enters -
surely with a message?

Millions look up
from blank hills, quiet suburban gardens:
and here you stand,
binoculars trained to the sky
wondering why this comet
tells of time opening out
like a fountain of light,

embracing Halley,
your grandfather in nineteen ten,
and all the people
gathered together
on the edge of the arena,
where time slides
under black arches of space.

The messenger has taken
seventy-five years
to fly his predicted route.
You have not long to watch:
While Orion walks on, slow, haughty,
the message burns itself
in its own beautiful fire.

SEQUENCE ON THE CHINESE UPRISING: JUNE 1989

1. Student

She is out in the square,
Su, one of thousands,
a girl with long black hair
who tells the world she stands
for liberty, she will not eat or drink
for liberty. The crazed
tanks wait on the brink,
stopped by all the upraised
hands. Su waves to us,
then turns back to the Square.
Freedom is half-open like the lotus
flowering in her hair.

2. Statue

Last week, these art students
made abstract shapes
beautiful in space,
crafted their freedom
in wood, concrete, glass.

But freedom has become
a gathering of thousands,
a waving of flags.
Their statue of liberty
is hastily made.

She lacks strength,
invisible girders,
She is a bland copy.
Her unwieldy height
diminishes the crowd.

At night they unveil her
in Tiananmen Square.
She is without expression,
a tall mannequin
waiting to be clothed.

3. Peasant Soldier

The peasant soldier is on the move,
One two, one two.
What can a boy of sixteen prove?
One two, one two.
His innocent mouth is open wide,
One two, one two,
Only a month from his mother's side,
One two, one two.
He shakes the hands of the student crowd,
One two, one two.
He does not mean to laugh outloud,
One two, one two.
Or weep on the barrel of his gun,
One two, one two,
Or lose his head in the Peking sun,
One two, one two,
Or stumble on, or stumble on...

4. The Leaf

Alone, deliberately,
with bare hands raised,
the student makes a dance,
his rain dance in a parched land.

The convoy crawls
from left to right, then stops.
The young man leaps
onto the leading tank

to tell the driver
Freedom is only a handshake away.
The soldier hesitates,
like a man caught in rain.

Sure as gunfire,
cameras click. Next day,
The student holds up the world
with his raised hand.

5. Hell

Night invades the square, the rain holds off.
Stars are clouded, candles and torches gleam.
Goodnight, goodnight.

An old lady brings us soap and water.
We wash our shirts, we lie quietly
and dream of liberty.

At first it is thunder, a break in the weather.
Then someone screams, 'They are coming,
they are firing!'

Tanks roll on as if we are not there.
Another calls, 'I am twenty, I have no mother!'
We cry for peace.

We cry, we lift our hands, our bare faces,
But Hell drives down into the Square, rolls us
down into the dark earth.

6. Aftermath

The curfew sounds,
bonfires litter the city.
An old lady in black
weeps into her hand.

Trails of smoke
become a cloud,
become the sky,
become nothing.

At these cremations
there is no gathering.
No lessons are read.
No-one sings.

This morning's silence
is rage, is pity,
is fear, is impotence,
is the bonfire of the heart.

7. Grief

Only grief for mankind's grieving heart
can set the Devil and Mankind apart.

8. Symbols

Darkness falls.
Oblivion is more powerful than freedom.

Moon rises.
Symbols are more potent than oblivion.

They shine,
Their distant movement turns the tide.

Or buried deep,
Their green blades cut the winter earth like leaves.

On Henry Moore's Shelter Drawing

These are not Londoners
huddled below
huge explosions,
search lights,
burning trees.

They are from an underworld
whose tunnels lead us back
to Orpheus and further back
to archaic burial chambers
where we all sleep.

In the wounded morning
this rabble will rise
from the London underground
and re-assemble
in other pictures, whose beauty

will also encompass destruction.
Simple, eternal,
these figures sleep
in the strange hole
that lies under every city.

Winter Earthquake

Fingers walk like a spider
between concrete blocks,
explore the crack then suddenly withdraw
and step again into white holy air
to touch the hands of the world.

Into the dark Armenian winter
pilgrims come: rulers, shepherds,
firemen, engineers, bearing gifts.
There is little to salvage
in the skeleton of this city

yet even those who cannot leave for grief
tear at the concrete crib with bare hands.
After ten days they prise her free:
An old Armenian lady
in weekday clothes.

Tonight the moon shines
on her upturned city,
snow falls, unknown shadows wander.
By her broken crib a fire for the homeless
burns like a fallen star.

Last Letters in the War Museum, Brittany

Simply, with no cleverness,
how else to write on the last breath
at twenty-one? 'Do not be sad,'
he wrote, 'I am condemned to death.

I die tomorrow. Do not grieve.
I go with courage having done
my duty. *Bien chers parents,*
give my love to everyone.'

Another wrote: 'My brother has
been shot; three other brothers are
held prisoner. They will come back
to be with you after the war.'

For offering resistance these
young men have won a little fame.
Visitors to the museum
lean across the glass to claim

a personal meaning from the words
written with odd, schoolboy grace,
and linger, open-mouthed, as if
the heart of war lies in the case.

The Camp, West Beirut

The road is dry, mud flakes into air.
Children wait with open silent mouths
and watch the soldiers shoot their daily bread.
A little way away food lorries slump
like prehistoric beasts. Gunshot dust
spreads and filters in the sun like rust.

Dreams of war have made the children less
than human, or a soldier would run back
with bowls of rice. Nor can we walk the road:
The camera man who shows us where to go
is in the way - he shoots another dream:
the children float and fall into the screen.

As we switch the television off
the picture dwindles to a needle point.
Voices halt, the screen reverts to grey.
But somewhere, far behind, the children wait
with open, silent mouths. The blind is down.
War falls like rain and all their childhoods drown.

War Child

Do not bury me alive,
trail me down grey roads
that lead nowhere.
Do not turn my tree into a green explosion
or lop off my fingers and toes -
they are dancers,
they obey a thousand commands a day.
Do not pour metal over my field,
it is alive, blue flowers
chime under my feet.
Do not make me so guarded
I forget where I put my secrets,
or make me hide for so long
I can no longer find myself.

Lebanon

Beside the road
harvest stubble burns
- wild flowers of fire.
Wind is in the scented smoke - a wayward
mounting genie of the flames that turns
the sky above the pyre
to grey falling shards.

But elsewhere air
is water-silk and bright:
There sun easily
floats like a golden buoy on the horizon.
Over my swinging road the moon is white -
still water-lily
in grey leaves of evening.

I drive on listening
to the distant news:
It pulls the night earth round.
Sad Lebanon unshrouds its massacre.
What voice does justice to those born to lose,
whose sky has fallen down
fallen down forever?

Another harvest burns
and darkness hangs the air.
Its field is a red riot:
Its flames are hands stuck in the ground that stir
and stir and cannot reach the high
domain of lost quiet.
The moon in her still water.

Light a Candle Tonight

Light a candle tonight:
Maria Colwell is dead
Killed by her stepfather.
When man and evil wed
No words can be said.
Light a candle tonight.

Light a candle tonight:
Tyra Henry is cold
Savaged by her father,
Twenty-one months old,
her childhood bought and sold.
Light a candle tonight.

Light a candle tonight:
Kimberly has gone,
Struck by her stepfather,
Starved to skin and bone.
Silent as a stone.
Light a candle tonight.

Light a candle tonight
for others, the unknown:
Across their little beds
The devil's fur has grown.
Their dreams are not their own.
Light a candle tonight.

The Old Campaigner

I am an old campaigner in this war:
One thing is certain, they will not break loose.
They cover up their tracks with care before
They turn a man's coat sleeves into a noose.
I am an old campaigner in this war.

Their eyes will blindly shine when they throw stones,
As if they are bombarding him with flowers.
Don't be surprised: they do not hear his groans,
But the insistent countdown of his hours.
Their eyes will blindly shine when they throw stones.

They have their answer, why they can watch pain.
They'll try to blindfold you in the same haze.
Like Peter Pan they do not live to gain
Some understanding but to arrest their days.
They have their answer why they can watch pain.

They camouflage their passion with strange lies
And proudly wear the medals of deception.
They are what they no longer recognise,
So they are fearful of their own reception.
They camouflage their passion with strange lies.

I am an old campaigner in this war,
But now I take my leave of this torn land.
I too am wounded by the things I saw
And I must heal my wounds to understand.
I am an old campaigner in this war.

Imprints

Imprint

Rain silks the beach,
sun drizzles.
In such weather
memory draws the eye.

Once in the rain
at Lyme Regis
you picked up a fossil
embedded in stone,
untouched by earth weather,
a perfect imprint
from the rain forest:

Your brown hand held
a small eternity.

Today, your image
un-nets time.
I hold you close and clear
in the long rain.
You, and the tag
of brightly coloured children
on the wet beach.

Encounter

We round the corner:
Geese run in the road,
their back yard has no border.
Ducks officially parade.

Yellow ducklings huddle, head to tail.
By the ancient farmhouse, hung with flowers
the sandy pond is frilled with mud.
An old lady, leaning on her broom

looks up and smiles.
She wears immemorial black
and time slips back -
is she her mother or her grandmother?

We are only passing, passing,
yet by the way the children
stop and stare,
one holding a small flower in his fist,

the other a great fern,
they too become part of the scene, part
of every summer childhood lost in time
or hidden by a turning in the road.

The Wink

At low tide on the estuary
crinkled water basks in mud
like a crocodile.
Where seagulls swing in widening arcs,
the sky retreats.
Along looped beaches sea smells hover,

grasses spike, pebbles gleam in sand.
A child gathers rainbow stones
for her red pail,
then stares accross the silky mud:
It is time
for the water ceremony. It is time

for the water to open one eye
and look at her. Long after
her rainbow stones have lost
their evocative shine
the water's wink
will moisten her mind's eye.

From the Museum Window

Meadows are upturned, wefts of clumsy
mud dry the horizon. An earth mover
ducks and scoops. Low down in the sky
a flag of birds dips. White clouds hover.

The archeologist hurries like an ant.
He has a few more days to dig his black
hole collapsing on the past.
Only the museum guards his stack
of pots and pans. His Roman citadel
will be a runway for the shining hoards
of supercranes that may pull down the moon.
'The moon,' you echo and I turn towards

you, staring, transfixed by a round and silver
plate in a glass case, and know your childhood
smile is of a timeless present I
have lost, another moon caught in a cupboard.

The Leap

Rising three, teetering on toes,
Looking me full in the eye,
Wary but giving me
the benefit of the doubt,
running back and coming
like a bullet from a gun -

you leap into my arms:
and I in the water
wait to show you
that jumping a long way
into a pool where you might sink
is a way of saying yes to life.

My Italian Cherub

Running naked, brown, little pot belly,
hair black, soft as down,
dark eyes clear, light-hearted,

you are my Italian cherub.
I imagine, just for once,
life will do you a favour.

Look what you offer - a willing heart,
an alert mind, bare feet
that run without fear.

I want you to be suspended
in a crook of time, offered a pause,
a green place to dance.

But you run into the cross-current
of human disfavour.
They say no-one is to blame.

Enemies are in your camp,
they quietly go about
cutting the grass under your feet.

So I must keep you in mind, as Della Robbia
put you in the choir stall, Botticelli
left you laughing, high up in a blue sky.

Moon Joy

Do not listen
when they tell you
the moon is barren.

It is an old wives' tale.
Round, bold
her influence is pale

yet everywhere apparent:
trees are moon-bare.
earth transparent,

every blade of grass
bears the mystery
of outer space,

every flower
wears her still
white power.

Look, even my hair,
even my lifted hands
share her.

So do not listen
when they tell you
the moon is barren,

do not lose your trust:
Child of the universe,
her message is light, not dust.

White Stones

Air presses down,
hot hand.
vipers hide in dry grass
plants shrivel.

Only the white stones
are cool and uncompromising,
worked and placed by men
who knew their healing.
They wait in the shadow
of six thousand years.

We cannot feel
their sacred
inner rhythm.

Yet their cold white touch
comforts us.
Tomorrow the rain will come.

Breakdown

The boy flew out of his window, light as air.
Who came in that night?
A giant doll with a broken stare,
stuffed with soot.
His legs folded, gave, would not hold,
so he rolled
over and over, arms above his head
beside the bed.
The light of the room went out and low
rain plundered the window.

When lightfoot Mrs. Moppet came
next day to tidy up the room -
'Where is my boy?' she cried,
and 'What is this?' She tried
to stir the giant doll but there
was no life in his spine or stare.
'What an untidy carry-on,' she sighed,
for little piles of soot were everywhere.
Filled with a spring of sorrow for this hump
of a doll lolling in a trance,

lightfoot Mrs. Moppet did a dance
over his bed - hop, skip, jump!
At last a spot of light - tip of a needle
lit up the doll's blank eyes. 'Speed well'
sang Mrs. Moppet. Everyday, inspired,
she capered over the bed waving
her yellow mop, dancing on
feathers of faith,
until one morning faith flew out of her soul
and fired her yellow mop held high.

(Cont.)

Breakdown (Cont.)

Strangely it shone
like a huge sparkler, like a giant star
lifting the room to white.
Out of his black garden came the boy:
Over his shoulder, through the window, he put
the doll, who floated away in a shower of soot.
Only then did the light die down
and the boy come into his own.
'My!' said Mrs. Moppet, smiling at her son,
'This is more like home.'

Moving On

They took a long time to collect, posters
of baby-faced Paul, John Lennon,
the astronaut who with a little step
turned moon-man into dust, and here are other
space gods of your childhood, coming home,
their parachutes like flowers on the sea.

You made your own mission in the attic,
left your moon dust on the beams, litter
only you can decode in the cupboard:
coke cans, letters folded into eight,
a scarf of many colours never worn,
little china ornaments and frog

who sat one winter in a toyshop window
and taught you unrequited love, and love.
Badges of your worldly exploits lie
around: I CAN DO SEX NOW   I HAVE SEEN
THE LIONS OF LONGLEAT but not discarded:
The attic guards this last night audience.

Above the table marked with coffee rings
night no longer charts a fairy place.
Stars are labelled, footsteps mark the moon,
the window opens on a waiting world.
But frog is going blind with dust, and will
your parachute grow flowers as you leap?

Painting De Hooch

A door half open, a child stands
in a passage of sunlight.
Nothing overrules the quiet:
it folds over the nurse,
the baby in a wooden rocking cradle.
They are transformed like beautifully painted drapery
into the material of silence.
Future and past lie in the open door
but the child waits, waits
for nothing at all.

Leave-Taking

One-eyed Pete

He cannot see straight,
that is the long and the short of it.
Once he had a belly
round as a mushroom top
and two twinkly eyes.
Now he only has one eye.
It filters everything.

Grey. Grey. Poor one-eyed Pete.
He has forgotten why people laugh.
When you laugh he smiles sadly.
His trousers wash round him,
his hands clasp together.
when he lies down,
he prays to his one-eyed god.

But you should see him dressed for work!
A handkerchief in his pocket,
a lavender expression on his face.
In his laundered suit
he fights the lions and tigers.
A jackal is at his throat -
He does not give up -

though he has been known
to shut his office door
and sleep and sleep.
Does anyone know the cure for one-eyed Pete?
He cannot go on much longer -
the world is shrinking
into a small, black stone.

Poem for Sally (1)

You're playing games with me; soon you will rise
with mischief in your eyes.
When we were little it was so -
playing at being dead.

Here by your bed
life is all uncluttered - not even talk;
only the dream I had where you lay down
as you are now, so beautiful and pale,
lies in my mind.
Is it another dream that brings you here
to quietly unveil
the lost clarity, the hidden vigil
of your own love? Sybil
of the last flame!

Soon you will, you will
stop this strange game,
wake and walk into the park.
Not drift slowly into the deep dark.

But no, and since love can
- unmarred by thought or plan -
go with you to the border
in peace and order,
you do not have my tears.
Love overwhelms all fears.

So I sit calmly by you for this while.
Yet surely, soon, you will sit up and smile?

Poem for Sally (2)

We have nearly reached the end of the journey;
we have gone hand in hand.
Now I must wish you well, we've reached the border.
I have no passport to this land.
But spirit has no here and there,
no leave-taking, no loss.
So all my love and peace go with you -
since they will walk across.

Watercress Day
For Joss

Surprisingly they have been here
a long time, water meadows
fresh as rain, watercress
exotic like plants behind glass.
Along the patchwork river sun and cloud
float level with the grass.

Only the shack is derelict,
its owner out of sight, having
a trust in threadbare time -
He left his first clue years ago: across
the wall his roughly painted letters lean:
20p for water cress.

He made a dented metal hole
to take our coins. Do we wade
in wet meadows, pick his cress
like wild flowers? An arrow turns the rest
of the old wall into a treasure chart.
It points down to a chest.

We lift the lid: between metal
linings, watercress
sparkles like jewellery.
We post our silver coins, bearing in mind
the trust the owner has in us - then leave
his hidden world behind -

not without posting messages
of friendship into flowers, trees
and the receiving river.
and later when you trust me with your own
book, I find your life between its covers,
hidden and fresh as if it had been sewn,

(Cont.)

Watercress Day (Cont.)

gathered on our watercress day;
and evergreen the time you stood
alone in Winchester Cathedral,
with no pretence to live by, no address;
yet turned to hear God's voice and see his lost
meadows in the wilderness.

Leave-Taking

You who are dying and pick flowers
Walk the garden like an ambassador
Who knows a little more than us.
We do not talk of the country
Where you are going,
Where we are all going.

You bend over the blue delphiniums.
For a moment the flowers in your hands
Shields us from each other.
Rainlight spatters the lawn,
The pool is green with sedge,
Trees shadow the water.

You step down from the bank to the cool lawn.
The beauty of your flowers illuminates:
They are tall, an unbelievable blue,
They lie in my arms like flames,
The high blue torch of death.
Will they set fire to my heart?

It is difficult to imagine their petals
Lying on stone, downbeaten by the rain.
I cradle them into the car and wave.
We have no need for words:
It is a simple thing,
the coming and the going.

Song of the Lost Children

Where are the lonely children
With no leaves in their hair?
They stretch behind tall trees
Invisible as air.
All the time they whisper, whisper,
'We are here.'

Where are the troubled children
With no flowers in their hands?
They stand by the white wayside
Where the high thistle stands.
All the time they whisper, whisper,
'Make no demands.'

Where are the cruel children
With no sun in their eyes?
They crouch down in a ditch where
The mould of winter lies.
All the time they whisper, whisper,
'We will not rise.'

Where are the muted children
With no breath on the wind?
They lie like buried boulders
In the coffin of my mind.
All the time they whisper, whisper,
'We were all blind.'

Elaine

It's party night.
She's over eighty now:
poems and stories
of her family
hang on her memory
like the rainbow row
of garments she put out
on washing day:

She takes the floor to dance:
diminutive,
she tips her legs,
angles up her hands,
and like a little child
whose up too late,
defiantly,
she does the hornpipe dance.

The Measure of all Things

Four days before you died
I sat beside your bed.
Love and faith floated
like flowers between us,

like flowers on a sea
green with sunlight.
We watched them keep afloat:
For a quarter of an hour

everything was simple.
Then we kissed goodbye.
Your eyes shone like sunlight.
As I closed the door

Our farewell slipped away,
The sea grew dark. It was
a time from which to take
the measure of all things.

The Way the Old Sing

My neighbour does not sing
to be heard: hers
is a soft sound,
a bee humming,
wayward, persistent
settling into a tune,
a childhood ballad.

My father says singing
is good for the morale.
He remembers the words.
They are always about love.
His voice goes up and down,
like a bird that rides
a raging sea.

For old age seeps
into every nook and cranny:
Only his song escapes.

No Crutches

You do not want crutches or a zimmer
or any other contraption! You prefer
old sticks placed about the house, a kitchen
broom - bristling crutch - under your arm

to take you to the window where you lean,
- a prisoner behind glass - and watch the weather
ride the peachy light of dawn, or land
at night in the surprising wood of stars.

Today you stand on dying limbs: a wind
drives down your crooked trees, the sun is fluted,
haloed, like the daffodils I picked
to fill the jam jar on the window sill.

As you shuffle round to face the yellow
ragged garden sun, I half expect
you to take off and die this way, riding
into the rough and tumble of the spring.

A Long Way

I am a long way from last week,
the chair where you gathered bluebells, primroses,
walked by the sea,
where you tested your deaf aid with
'To be or not to be.'

A wind keens the Devon lowland,
over Sheepwash
skies billow, pleat rain,
break into the blue hush of summer.
A hundred poems blossom from this house
but only birds sing certainly of Spring.

I would like to tell you
the pathway where I walk is all in bloom.
But I am a long way from last week,
and you will never know
the flowers I pick to decorate our table
are primroses and bluebells from your garden.

The Hare

He is high on danger,
trembles upright,
eyes blank with fear,
ears tipped to catch the rumble of feet
in snow that tumbles like an acrobat
across the field.
Defeated, the hare drops, circles away
into the bent grass.

But when the artist
holds him up by the ears,
danger does not unbalance him.
Inside the well-lit gallery
where people circle round and round,
cumbersome, hidden in their clothes,
dangerous,
his fear is in a trance:
the bronze hare stands on two feet,
naked acrobat.

The Snowdrop

Darkness is not endemic,
black end of year lifts
leaving only a small trace
of damp-dun undergrowth, brown bracken
along the railway line,
the country road.

A fresh light stretches.
leaves flicker and flash
like green memories.
Out of clumsy soil a snowdrop slips,
filling my garden
with forgotten possibilities.

The Edge of Things

A SEQUENCE: EARTH, AIR, FIRE, WATER

Earth: The Track

This earth is many toe'd -
Footprints cross like star on star,
Down the woodland track
Man dances on the dinosaur.
Alpha and Omega.

Rain pools reflect the sun
With shining skirts awry, but mire
And heavy chalk weigh down
Earth's dark inner fire.
Alpha and Omega.

This untilled ground is green seed
And graveyard; stones that are
Like flaked skeletons
Bring winter woods to flower.
Alpha and Omega.

For earth is alchemy's stone.
Lost, somewhere, on the Milky Way,
A little ball of dust
And Michelangelo's clay.
Alpha and Omega.

Kingdoms are made from it,
But when its time of fostering
Is over, earth deposes
Every kingdom, every king.
Alpha and Omega.

Air: Landing

Across the cloud antarctica
snow shelf edges snow ridge; ice
flickers in feathers of light.
An airy precipice

suddenly shafts down
to fields in miniature.
Neat, green, brown
squares of watercolour.

Like a clockwork bird
our plane in rigid chains
of noise shadows the sunbird's dazzling flight,
then drops into snow mountains.

The crash is strange - is it mind turning impact
into cotton wool, rising tides of grey,
sunlost earth? In halflight
fields, trees, houses turn up the right way.

The plane lands on a concrete slab. We walk
an earth imprisoned by tarmac, tread
the slow escalator, half distracted
by posters of vaunted holidays

in the sun. But we are haunted
by the sunbird, in his brilliant white
domain of light, who, like a hunter, tracks
eternity in an unending flight.

Fire: Winter Hearth

In the mauve winter
Child, daughter, mother
Sit by the hearth and stare
At flames walking on air:
Other fires burn there.

In ash's powder
And pulsing glow, crowd the
Images of a room,
Half light, half gloom
where lost childhoods bloom.

But the child on the couch
Keeps a different watch
On the flames, searching
For a great lion crouching,
A world waiting to spring.

Water: The Seaside Man

You are the salt man:
Along the Sussex beach
quiet men and women
sing in your speech.

Ancient tribes spring off
your mind, leaping
across this silent cliff
in the white nose of the wind.

You are the rock man:
You point to the beautiful
trees that grow where green
empires slid into rubble,

and know that stars, sprigs of may,
sea foam, daisies in the grass
have white nets that will always
cover the black abyss.

You are the sand man:
Here at the rim of England
the sea's cool calligraphy
marks the sand

and you often stand, comforted
where England changes shape and swings
into water. You are not afraid
of the edge of things.

Reflection on Cathy's Tiger Painted in Glass

(Royal College of Art Diploma Show)

Trammelled in glass
painted tiger prowls.
Squibs of coloured grass
shoot from his tail,
clouds of milky fog
close round his soft
and dangerous head.
We see at eye level
our own cool heads impaled
on quick silver, our watchful
eyes the painted glass
where swift thoughts skate
like spindly flies passed up
from some lost place
within, inviolate.
The jungle where our tigers pace.

Cave Painting

Out of the blackness, a signal:
Horse with the carved muzzle
and charcoal eye, you are
the mark of a man who saw
a wild, white horse in flight
and painted it out of sight,
marking it above
with stencilled hands. What drove

that man here, where no
river flowed, only its hollow
outline? How did he guess
in silence and in darkness
the pillar of time grows slow
and strong like stalagmite? So
kingdoms of time pause
in the dark eye of his horse.

What other horse does the earth
hide, running the cave
of time for an invisible
painter, bearing his signal:
Deep as the root of an old tree, bright
as a winter star, but like starlight
reflecting a past the mind sees
but cannot recognise.

The Heartlands of Poetry

When shadow is
the sun's dark kiss

and blossom, falling, blowing
is every fresh remembered thing.

When the moon's face
is the beauty of all space

and the amazing stars
burn down prison bars.

When pain, on its knees,
offers unimagined ease

and the movement of one finger
is an example of wonder.

When footprints left about
turn the heart inside out.

then you go free
into the heartlands of poetry